DiscoverRoo
An Imprint of Pop!
popbooksonline.com

Cultural Celebrations

SPRING EQUINOX

by Elizabeth Andrews

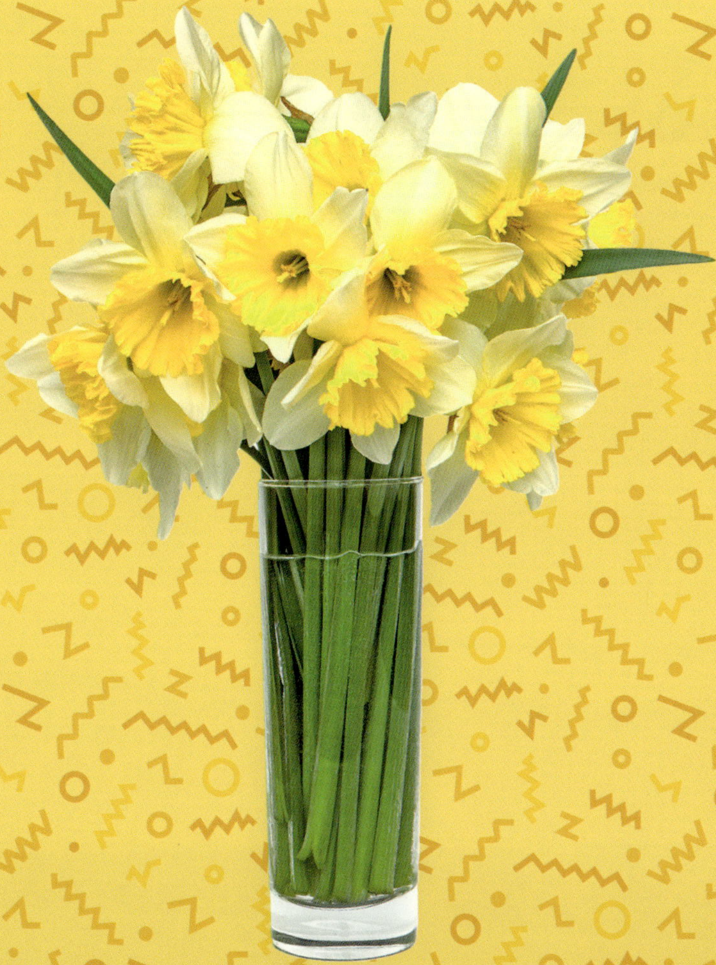

WELCOME TO DiscoverRoo!

This book is filled with videos, puzzles, games, and more! Scan the QR codes* while you read, or visit the website below to make this book pop.

popbooksonline.com/spring-eqx

abdobooks.com

Published by Pop!, a division of ABDO, PO Box 398166, Minneapolis, Minnesota 55439. Copyright © 2024 by Abdo Consulting Group, Inc. International copyrights reserved in all countries. No part of this book may be reproduced in any form without written permission from the publisher. DiscoverRoo™ is a trademark and logo of Pop!.

Printed in the United States of America, North Mankato, Minnesota.

102023
012024

THIS BOOK CONTAINS RECYCLED MATERIALS

Cover: Shutterstock Images
Interior: Shutterstock Images; Getty Images; Wikimedia Commons
Editor: Emily Dreher
Series Designer: Colleen McLaren

Library of Congress Control Number: 2023939064

Publisher's Cataloging-in-Publication Data
Names: Andrews, Elizabeth, author.
Title: Spring Equinox / by Elizabeth Andrews
Description: Minneapolis, Minnesota : Pop!, 2024 | Series: Cultural celebrations | Includes online resources and index
Identifiers: ISBN 9781098245399 (lib. bdg.) | ISBN 9781098245955 (ebook)
Subjects: LCSH: Spring festivals--Juvenile literature. | Vernal equinox--Juvenile literature. | Holidays--Juvenile literature. | Cultural sociology--Juvenile literature.
Classification: DDC 394.26--dc23

*Scanning QR codes requires a web-enabled smart device with a QR code reader app and a camera.

TABLE OF CONTENTS

CHAPTER 1
First Spring Morning 4

CHAPTER 2
History of the Spring Equinox 8

CHAPTER 3
Spiritual Spring 14

CHAPTER 4
Spring Equinox Around
the World 22

Making Connections. 30
Glossary 31
Index. 32
Online Resources 32

CHAPTER 1

FIRST SPRING MORNING

Evan wakes up early on the morning of March 20th. He looks outside and sees the sun beginning to peek over the trees. He hears the *drip, drip, drip* of last night's rain falling from the roof. It's going to be a beautiful spring equinox.

WATCH A VIDEO HERE!

The morning of the spring equinox is usually chilly. The day often gets warmer in the afternoon.

Woods are good places to look for the first signs of spring.

Evan and his family dress in warm clothes. They are going on a sunrise walk through their favorite path in the woods. They take this walk every year on the equinox. As they wander the path, his dad points out newly growing plants and busy birds.

When Evan and his family get home, they gather at the kitchen table. His mother sets out spring equinox decorations. There are the painted eggs and bunny figures along with a vase of fresh flowers. As a family, they spend their breakfast talking about all the warm-weather activities they are looking forward to. They give thanks to nature for bringing back the light and warmth after a long winter.

Daffodils and peonies are popular spring flowers.

CHAPTER 2

HISTORY OF THE SPRING EQUINOX

The spring equinox happens on March 20th or 21st in the Northern **Hemisphere**. On this day, the hours of sunlight are equal to the hours of darkness. An equinox occurs twice a year when the sun is exactly over the equator. Until the first day of summer, each day after the spring equinox has more hours of sunlight.

LEARN MORE HERE!

WHAT IS AN EQUINOX?

Earth's axis is slightly tilted. The tilt causes seasons.

When a hemisphere is tilted toward the sun, days are longer and warmer.

When a hemisphere is tilted away from the sun, days are shorter and colder.

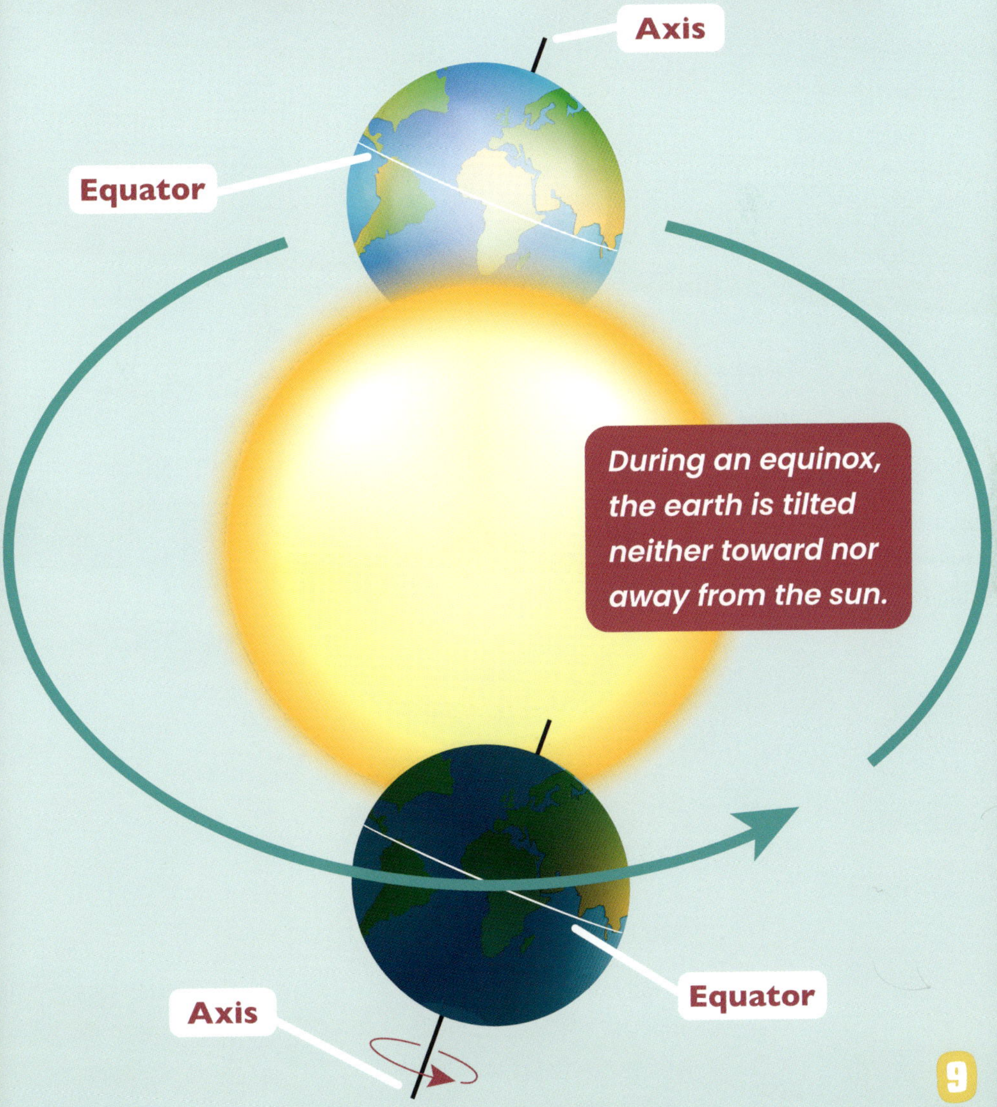

Axis

Equator

During an equinox, the earth is tilted neither toward nor away from the sun.

Equator

Axis

Bison are native to the Badlands of South Dakota. They were an important food source for the Lakota.

>
> **DID YOU KNOW?**
> The **Lakota** people knew it was time to move to higher land during the spring equinox. They followed the bison herds.

Thousands of years ago, humans kept track of time with the sun's shadow and the phases of the moon. They also paid attention to **astronomical** events. An equinox is an example of an astronomical event. When the spring equinox happened, humans knew it was time to start planting food for the coming year.

A sundial tells the time based on where the sun casts its shadow.

Once the harvesting was done, it was time to start preparing the earth for planting again.

Before modern society, human life revolved around farming. People had to work very hard to get the earth ready for planting. Then they had to work hard planting and caring for food as it grew. After growing through the spring and summer, food was ready to **harvest**.

The spring equinox was a very exciting time for these humans. It meant they made it through the harsh winter. When spring came, so did warmth and light. Animal babies would be born soon, and plants would start growing. People connected spring to new life.

People fill Roman streets to celebrate spring in the painting *Spring* by Lawrence Alma-Tadema

CHAPTER 3
SPIRITUAL SPRING

People have been celebrating the spring equinox for thousands of years all over the world. In Europe, before Christianity spread, people believed in many gods and **worshipped** nature. The changing of seasons held great **spiritual** meaning.

EXPLORE LINKS HERE!

One spring equinox celebration from long ago that is still celebrated today is called Ostara. Ostara is a festival honoring the loss of winter and appearance of spring. It was named after the German **goddess** of spring, Eostre.

Spring goddesses are shown in famous works of art such as Primavera by Sandro Botticelli.

It is difficult to learn exactly how ancient people practiced their **rituals**. They had no written language. Traditions were passed down orally. Some **scholars** believe the hare was Eostre's **sacred** animal. Other scholars connect Eostre's hares with Easter. Easter is a Christian holiday held in the spring. *Eostre* is where the word *Easter* came from.

Hares are animals similar to rabbits.

One story of Eostre states that she turned a bird into a hare. This is why eggs are often seen with hares in equinox decorations.

Some ancient nature worshippers were called druids. There are still druids around the world today. On the spring equinox, they celebrate Alban Eilir. *Alban Eilir* means "Light of the Earth." Druids believe one of their goddesses, the Spring Maiden, sleeps during the winter. She awakens on the spring equinox.

> **Druids lived in areas that became modern day United Kingdom, Ireland, and France.**

Churches and homes are sometimes decorated with images of the Green Man.

Modern druids hold rituals to celebrate Alban Eilir. They light black and white candles to represent the balance of sunlight and darkness. They give thanks to the Spring Maiden for the warmth she brings. They also thank their god the Green Man. He is the god of plant life and brings about new life lessons.

The Triple Goddess is represented by a full moon and two crescent moons.

Today, people who celebrate Ostara and Alban Eilir honor the festivals in different ways. They spend time in nature by taking a walk or hike. They observe nature changing around them. They may also meditate and plant seeds. Some people make altars in their homes. They may decorate altars with important plants, images, stones, and candles.

Some people gather altar decorations on nature walks.

CHAPTER 4
SPRING EQUINOX AROUND THE WORLD

The spring equinox has happened since Earth was formed. It's likely been celebrated since the first human communities. This long history can be seen in beautiful **architecture** around the world.

COMPLETE AN ACTIVITY HERE!

Angkor Wat is a large group of temples in Cambodia. On the equinox, the sun rises directly over the center lotus tower.

One of the most famous examples of architecture that honors the spring equinox is the Pyramid of Kukulcán in the Maya site Chichén Itzá. The pyramid is dedicated to the serpent god Kukulcán. Every year on the equinox a serpent appears to be coming down the steps. The "serpent" is the zigzag shadow cast by the steps. It meets the serpent head statue at the bottom of the pyramid by 4:30 p.m.

The Pyramid of Kukulcán was built between 1050 and 1300 CE.

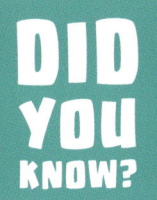

DID YOU KNOW? The Maya knew it was time to plant maize when the serpent came down the temple.

People from all over come to see the serpent. There is a viewing platform where nearly 10,000 people sit to watch the serpent appear. The Maya had the most advanced **astronomical** understanding of their time.

The Pueblo people built the structures in Chaco Canyon.

In New Mexico, there are structures from the Pueblo people dating back 1,200 years. In the ceremonial chamber of Casa Rinconada, the sun climbs the walls every day. During sunrise on the spring equinox, the sun shines directly through two doorways, landing in a small indent in the wall.

Highly advanced ancient societies created architecture.

The spring equinox celebrates rebirth and renewal. People around the world use it to mark the beginning of a new year. Persians begin their Nowruz holiday

People celebrate Nowruz in Afghanistan, India, Kazakhstan, Pakistan, Turkey, and Uzbekistan

on the spring equinox. They clean their homes and leap over fires. No matter where it is celebrated, the first day of spring comes with a lot of joy.

MAKING CONNECTIONS

TEXT-TO-SELF

Anyone can celebrate the spring equinox! If you celebrated the equinox, how would you spend your day?

TEXT-TO-TEXT

Have you read any books about another celebration that happens in the spring? If so, how was it similar to or different from equinox celebrations?

TEXT-TO-WORLD

This book mentions beautiful places around the world to view the spring equinox. Where would you like to visit to celebrate the equinox? Please explain your answer.

GLOSSARY

architecture — the art of planning and designing buildings.

astronomical — of or relating to the study of anything outside of Earth's atmosphere.

harvest — to gather a crop.

hemisphere — one half of Earth divided at the equator. Earth has a Northern and Southern Hemisphere.

Lakota — one of the original peoples who lived in the Great Plains of the United States.

ritual — a spiritual action performed in a certain way.

sacred — connected with worship of a god.

scholar — a person who has deeply studied a specific subject.

spiritual — having to do with religious matters or people's beliefs in things, such as the soul, nature, or what happens after death

worship — to show love, respect, and affection to an object, person, or being.

INDEX

Alban Eilir, 18–20
animals, 6–7, 13, 16
architecture, 22, 24–25, 27

Casa Rinconada, 27

druids, 18–19

Eostre, 15–16
Europe, 14

farming, 11–12

gods and goddesses, 14–16, 18–19, 24

hemisphere, 8

Maya, 24–25

nature, 6–7, 18–21
New Mexico, 27

Ostara, 15, 20

Persians, 28
Pyramid of Kukulcán, 24–25

rituals, 19–21, 29

sun, 4, 8, 9, 11, 19, 27

warmth, 7, 13, 19

This book is filled with videos, puzzles, games, and more! Scan the QR codes* while you read, or visit the website below to make this book pop.

popbooksonline.com/spring-eqx

*Scanning QR codes requires a web-enabled smart device with a QR code reader app and a camera.